Aurora of the Philosophers

By

Paracelsus

ISBN: 978-1-63118-507-6

Esoteric Classics

Other Books in this Series and Related Titles

Paracelsus, the Four Elements and Their Spirits by M P Hall (978-1-63118-400-0)

Masonic and Rosicrucian History by M P Hall & H Voorhis (978-1-63118-486-4)

The Rosicrucian Chemical Marriage by Christian Rosenkreuz (978-1-63118-458-1)

The Influence of Pythagoras on Freemasonry and Other Essays (978-1-63118-404-8)

The Golden Verses of Pythagoras: Five Translations (978-1-63118-479-6)

Freemasonry, Mithraism and the Ancient Mysteries by various (978-1-63118-407-9)

History, Analysis and Secret Tradition of the Tarot by Hall &c (978-1-63118-445-1)

The Kabbalah of Masonry & Related Writings by E Levi &c (978-1-63118-453-6)

A Collection of Early Writings on Astral Travel (978-1-63118-477-2)

Masonic Symbolism of King Solomon's Temple by A Mackey &c (978-1-63118-442-0)

Buddhist Psalms by Shinran (978-1-63118-465-9)

Magical Essays and Instructions by Florence Farr (978-1-63118-418-5)

The Ceremony of Initiation: Analysis & Commentary (978-1-63118-473-4)

The Master Mason's Handbook by J S M Ward (978-1-63118-474-1)

The Old Past Master by Carl H Claudy (978-1-63118-464-2)

The Path of Light: A Manual of Maha-Yana Buddhism (978-1-63118-471-0)

The Hymns of Hermes by G. R. S. Mead (978-1-63118-405-5)

The Book of the Watchers by Enoch (978-1-63118-416-1)

The Lost Keys of Freemasonry or The Secret of Hiram Abiff (978-1-63118-427-7)

Catholicism, Yoga and Hinduism by Hartmann &c (978-1-63118-478-9)

American Indian Freemasonry by A C Parker (978-1-63118-460-4)

Ancient Mysteries and Secret Societies by M P Hall (978-1-63118-410-9)

Audio Versions are also available on Audible, Amazon and Apple

Other Books in this Series and Related Titles

The Devil in Love by Jacques Cazotte (978–1–63118–499–4)

Alchemy in the Nineteenth Century by Helena P. Blavatsky (978-1-63118-446-8)

Gnosis of the Mind by G. R. S. Mead (978-1-63118-408-6)

On the Cave of the Nymphs in the Odyssey by Thomas Taylor (978-1-63118-505-2)

Plato and Platonism and Related Esoteric Essays by various (978-1-63118-432-1)

Clairvoyance and Psychic Abilities by A Besant &c (978-1-63118-403-1)

The Book of Wisdom of Solomon by King Solomon (978-1-63118-502-1)

The Smoky God or A Voyage to the Inner World by Emerson (978-1-63118-423-9)

The Golden Verses of Pythagoras: Five Translations (978-1-63118-479-6)

Tao Te Ching & Commentary by Lao Tzu & C Johnston (978-1-63118-495-6)

The Magician's Heavenly Chaos by Thomas Vaughan (978-1-63118-500-7)

The Hymn of Jesus by G. R. S. Mead (978-1-63118-492-5)

Cloud Upon the Sanctuary by Waite & K Eckartshausen (978-1-63118-438-3)

Rosicrucian Rules, Secret Signs, Codes and Symbols by various (978-1-63118-488-8)

The Sepher Yetzirah and the Qabalah by M P Hall (978-1-63118-481-9)

Prashna Upanishad and Commentary by Charles Johnston (978-1-63118-494-9)

The Feminine Occult by various authors (978-1-63118-711-7)

The First and Second Gospels of the Infancy of Jesus Christ
by Thomas and James (978-1-63118-415-4)

The Machinery of the Mind by Dion Fortune (978-1-63118-451-2)

Brothers & Builders by Joseph Fort Newton (978-1-63118-506-9)

The Leadbeater Reader: A Selection of Occult Essays (978-1-63118-483-3)

Audio versions are also available on Audible, Amazon and Apple

Table of Contents

INTRODUCTION

The word "esoteric" can be difficult to define. Esotericism in general can be seen less as a system of beliefs and more as a category, which encompasses numerous, different systems of beliefs. It's a bit of juxtaposition, since the word "esoteric" indicates something that few people know about, while the term itself broadly covers numerous philosophies, practices, areas of study and belief systems.

In a greater sense, Esotericism acts as a storehouse for secret knowledge, which is often considered ancient *(by tradition, if not by fact),* passed down from generation to generation, in private. At various times in history, simply possessing the knowledge of some of these subjects, was considered illegal and a jailable offence, if discovered. This usually included such general topics as Alchemy, Pharmacology, Qabalah, Hermeticism, Occultism, Ceremonial Magic, Astrology, Divination, Rosicrucianism and so on. Collectively, these areas of study were often referred to as the esoteric sciences.

Sometimes, the outer garment of a subject isn't esoteric, while what is hidden beneath it, is. As an example, Freemasonry isn't necessarily esoteric by nature (at *least not anymore),* but certain signs, passwords and handshakes given to the candidate during their initiation, are in fact, esoteric, in the sense that they are hidden from the general public.

Today, in the twenty-first century, such topics are readily available at bookstores across the country, and numerous main-steam publishers offer beginners guides and coffee-table volumes on many of these subjects, intended for mass appeal. Books like "*The Secret*" have turned previously arcane topics into household knowledge. All that being the case, however, it isn't to say that there still aren't buried secrets to uncover, ancient wisdom being ignored and forgotten mysteries to be explored. In fact, it is often that we are only able to further our own studies by standing on the shoulders of these disappearing giants.

Lamp of Trismegistus is doing its part to help preserve humanity's esoteric history by making some of these classics available to those students who are seeking to unearth the knowledge of these ancient colossi.

So, be sure to check other titles from our *Esoteric Classics* series, as well as our *Occult Fiction*, *Theosophical Classics*, *Foundations of Freemasonry Series*, *Supernatural Fiction*, *Paranormal Research Series*, *Studies in Buddhism* and our *Christian Apocrypha Series.* You can also download the audio versions of most of these titles from Amazon, Apple or Audible, for learning on the go.

THE AURORA OF THE PHILOSOPHERS

BY THEOPHRASTUS PARACELSUS

WHICH HE OTHERWISE CALLS HIS MONARCHIA[1]

CHAPTER I

CONCERNING THE ORIGIN OF THE PHILOSOPHERS' STONE

Adam was the first inventor of arts, because he had knowledge of all things as well after the Fall as before.[2] Thence he predicted the world's destruction by water. From this cause, too, it came about that his successors erected two tables of stone, on which they engraved all natural arts in hieroglyphical characters, in order that their posterity might also become acquainted with this

[1] The work under this title is cited occasionally in other writings of Paracelsus, but is not included in the great folio published at Geneva in 1688. It was first issued at Basle in1575, and was accompanied with copious annotations in Latin by the editor, Gerard Dorne. This personage was a very persevering collector of the literary remains of Paracelsus, but is not altogether free from the suspicion of having elaborated his original. The Aurora is by some regarded as an instance in point; though no doubt in the main it is a genuine work of the Sage of Hohenheim, yet in some respects it does seem to approximate somewhat closely to previous schools of Alchemy, which can scarcely he regarded as representing the actual standpoint of Paracelsus.

[2] He who created man the same also created science. What has man in any place without labour? When the mandate went forth: Thou shalt live by the sweat of thy brow, there was, as it were, a new creation. When God uttered His fiat the world was made. Art, however, was not then made, nor was the light of Nature. But when Adam was expelled from Paradise, God created for him the light of Nature when He bade him live by the work of his hands. In like manner, He created for Eve her special light when He said to her: In sorrow shalt thou bring forth children. Thus, and there, were these beings made human and earthy that were before like angelicals. ... Thus, by the word were creatures made, and by this same word was also made the light which was necessary to man. ... Hence the interior man followed from the second creation, after the expulsion from Paradise. ... Before the Fall, that cognition which was requisite to man had not begun to develop in him. He received it from the angel when he was cast out of Paradise. ... Man was made complete in the order of the body, but not in the order of the arts. – De Caducis, Par. III.

prediction, that so it might be heeded, and provision made in the time of danger. Subsequently, Noah found one of these tables under Mount Araroth, after the Deluge. In this table were described the courses of the upper firmament and of the lower globe, and also of the planets. At length this universal knowledge was divided into several parts, and lessened in its vigour and power. By means of this separation, one man became an astronomer, another a magician, another a cabalist, and a fourth an alchemist. Abraham, that Vulcanic Tubalcain, a consummate astrologer and arithmetician, carried the Art out of the land of Canaan into Egypt, whereupon the Egyptians rose to so great a height and dignity that this wisdom was derived from them by other nations. The patriarch Jacob painted, as it were, the sheep with various colours; and this was done by magic: for in the theology of the Chaldeans, Hebrews, Persians, and Egyptians, they held these arts to be the highest philosophy, to be learnt by their chief nobles and priests. So it was in the time of Moses, when both the priests and also the physicians were chosen from among the Magi – the priests for the judgment of what related to health, especially in the knowledge of leprosy. Moses, likewise, was instructed in the Egyptian schools, at the cost and care of Pharaoh's daughter, so that he excelled in all the wisdom and learning of that people. Thus, too, was it with Daniel, who in his youthful days imbibed the learning of the Chaldeans, so that he became a cabalist. Witness his divine predictions and his exposition of those words, "Mene, Mene, Tecelphares". These words can be understood by the prophetic and cabalistic Art. This cabalistic Art was perfectly familiar to, and in constant use by, Moses and the Prophets. The Prophet Elias foretold many things by his cabalistic numbers. So did the Wise Men of old, by this natural and mystical Art, learn to know God rightly. They abode in His laws, and walked in His statutes with great firmness. It is also evident in the Book of Samuel, that the Berelists did not follow the devil's part, but became, by Divine permission, partakers of visions and veritable apparitions, whereof we shall treat more at large in the Book of Supercelestial Things.[3] This gift is granted by the Lord God to those priests who walk in the Divine precepts. It was a custom among the Persians never to admit any one as king unless he were a Wise Man, pre-eminent in reality as well as in name. This is clear from the customary name of their kings; for they were called Wise Men. Such were those Wise Men and Persian Magi who came from the East to seek out the Lord Jesus, and are called natural priests. The Egyptians, also, having obtained this magic and philosophy from the Chaldeans and Persians, desired that their priests should learn the same wisdom; and they became so fruitful and successful therein that all the neighbouring countries admired them. For this reason Hermes was so truly named Trismegistus, because he was a king, a priest, a prophet, a magician, and a sophist of natural things. Such another was Zoroaster.

[3] No work precisely corresponding co this title is extant among the writings of Paracelsus. The subjects to which reference is made are discussed in the Philosophia Sagax.

CHAPTER II

WHEREIN IS DECLARED THAT THE GREEKS DREW A LARGE PART OF THEIR LEARNING FROM THE EGYPTIANS; AND HOW IT CAME FROM THEM TO US

When a son of Noah possessed the third part of the world after the Flood, this Art broke into Chaldaea and Persia, and thence spread into Egypt. The Art having been found out by the superstitious and idolatrous Greeks, some of them who were wiser than the rest betook themselves to the Chaldeans and Egyptians, so that they might draw the same wisdom from their schools. Since, however, the theological study of the law of Moses did not satisfy them, they trusted to their own peculiar genius, and fell away from the right foundation of those natural secrets and arts. This is evident from their fabulous conceptions, and from their errors respecting the doctrine of Moses. It was the custom of the Egyptians to put forward the traditions of that surpassing wisdom only in enigmatical figures and abstruse histories and terms. This was afterwards followed by Homer with marvellous poetical skill; and Pythagoras was also acquainted with it, seeing that he comprised in his writings many things out of the law of Moses and the Old Testament. In like manner, Hippocrates, Thales of Miletus, Anaxagoras, Democritus, and others, did not scruple to fix their minds on the same subject. And yet none of them were practised in the true Astrology, Geometry, Arithmetic, or Medicine, because their pride prevented this, since they would not admit disciples belonging to other nations than their own. Even when they had got some insight from the Chaldeans and Egyptians, they became more arrogant still than they were before by Nature, and without any diffidence propounded the subject substantially indeed, but mixed with subtle fictions or falsehoods; and then they attempted to elaborate a certain kind of philosophy which descended from them to the Latins. These in their turn, being educated herewith, adorned it with their own doctrines, and by these the philosophy was spread over Europe. Many academies were founded for the propagation of their dogmas and rules, so that the young might be instructed; and this system flourishes with the Germans, and other nations, right down to the present day.

CHAPTER III

WHAT WAS TAUGHT IN THE SCHOOLS OF THE EGYPTIANS

The Chaldeans, Persians, and Egyptians had all of them the same knowledge of the secrets of Nature, and also the same religion. It was only the names that differed. The Chaldeans and Persians called their doctrine Sophia and Magic;[4] and the Egyptians, because of the sacrifice, called their wisdom priestcraft. The magic of the Persians, and the theology of the Egyptians, were both of them taught in the schools of old. Though there were many schools and learned men in Arabia, Africa, and Greece, such as Albumazar, Abenzagel, Geber, Rhasis, and Avicenna among the Arabians; and among the Greeks, Machaon, Podalirius, Pythagoras, Anaxagoras, Democritus, Plato, Aristotle, and Rhodianus; still there were different opinions amongst them as to the wisdom of the Egyptian on points wherein they themselves differed, and whereupon they disagreed with it. For this reason Pythagoras could not be called a wise man, because the Egyptian priestcraft and wisdom were not perfectly taught, although he received therefrom many mysteries and arcana; and that Anaxagoras had received a great many as well, is clear from his discussions on the subject of Sol and its Stone, which he left behind him after his death. Yet he differed in many respects from the Egyptians. Even they would not be called wise men or Magi; but, following Pythagoras, they assumed the name of philosophy: yet they gathered no more than a few gleams like shadows from the magic of the Persians and the Egyptians. But

[4] Before all things it is necessary to have a right understanding of the nature of Celestial Magic. It originates from divine virtue. There is that magic which Moses practised, and there is the maleficent magic of the sorcerers. There are, then, different kinds of Magi. So also there is what is called the Magic of Nature; there is the Celestial Magus; there is the Magus of Faith, that is, one whose faith makes him whole. There is, lastly, the Magus of Perdition. – Philosophia Sagax, Lib. II., c. 6.

Moses, Abraham, Solomon, Adam, and the wise men that came from the East to Christ, were true Magi, divine sophists and cabalists. Of this art and wisdom the Greeks knew very little or nothing at all; and therefore we shall leave this philosophical wisdom of the Greeks as being a mere speculation, utterly distinct and separate from other true arts and sciences.

CHAPTER IV

WHAT MAGI THE CHALDEANS, PERSIANS, AND EGYPTIANS WERE

Many persons have endeavoured to investigate and make use of the secret magic of these wise men; but it has not yet been accomplished. Many even of our own age exalt Trithemius, others Bacon and Agrippa, for magic and the cabala[5] – two things apparently quite distinct – not knowing why they do so. Magic, indeed, is an art and faculty whereby the elementary bodies, their fruits, properties, virtues, and hidden operations are comprehended. But the cabala, by a subtle understanding of the Scriptures, seems to trace out the way to God for men, to shew them how they may act with Him, and prophesy from Him; for the cabala is full of divine mysteries, even as Magic is full of natural secrets. It teaches of and foretells from the nature of things to come as well as of things present, since its operation consists in knowing the inner constitution of all creatures, of celestial as well as terrestrial bodies: what is latent within them; what are their occult virtues; for what they were originally designed, and with what properties they are endowed. These and the like subjects are the bonds wherewith things celestial are bound up with things of the earth, as may sometimes be seen in their operation even with the bodily eyes. Such a conjunction of celestial influences, whereby the heavenly virtues acted upon inferior bodies, was formerly called by the Magi a

---

[5] Learn, therefore, Astronomic Magic, which otherwise I call cabalistic. – De Pestilitate, Tract I. This art, formerly called cabalistic, was in the beginning named caballa, and afterwards caballia. It is a species of magic. It was also, but falsely, called Gabanala, by one whose knowledge of the subject was profound. It was of an unknown Ethnic origin, and it passed subsequently to the Chaldaeans and Hebrews, by both of whom it was corrupted. – Philosophia Sagax, Lib. I., s. v. Probatio in Scientiam Nectromantricam.

Gamahea,[6] or the marriage of the celestial powers and properties with elementary bodies. Hence ensued the excellent commixtures of all bodies, celestial and terrestrial, namely, of the sun and planets, likewise vegetables, minerals, and animals.

The devil attempted with his whole force and endeavour to darken this light; nor was he wholly frustrated in his hopes, for he deprived all Greece of it, and, in place thereof, introduced among that people human speculations and simple blasphemies against God and against His Son. Magic, it is true, had its origin in the Divine Ternary and arose from the Trinity of God. For God marked all His creatures with this Ternary and engraved its hieroglyph on them with His own finger. Nothing in the nature of things can be assigned or produced that lacks this magistery of the Divine Ternary, or that does not even ocularly prove it. The creature teaches us to understand and see the Creator Himself, as St. Paul testifies to the Romans. This covenant of the Divine Ternary, diffused throughout the whole substance of things, is indissoluble. By this, also, we have the secrets of all Nature from the four elements. For the Ternary, with the magical Quaternary, produces a perfect Septenary, endowed with many arcana and demonstrated by things which are known. When the Quaternary rests in the Ternary, then arises the Light of the World on the horizon of eternity, and by the assistance of God gives us the whole bond. Here also it refers to the virtues and operations of all creatures, and to their use, since they are stamped and marked with their arcana, signs, characters, and figures,

[6] The object which received the influence and exhibited the sign thereof appears to have been termed Gamaheu, Gamahey etc. But the name was chiefly given to certain stones on which various and wonderful images and figures of men and animals have been found naturally depicted, being no work of man, but the result of the providence and counsel of God. – De Imaginibus, c. 7 and c. 13. It is possible, magically, for a man to project his influence into these stones and some other substances. – Ibid., c. 13. But they also have their own inherent virtue, which is indicated by the shape and the special nature of the impression. – Ibid., c. 7. There was also an artificial Gamaheus invented and prepared by the Magi, and this seems to have been more powerful. – De Carduo Angelico.

so that there is left in them scarcely the smallest occult point which is not made clear on examination. Then when the Quaternary and the Ternary mount to the Denary is accomplished their retrogression or reduction to unity. Herein is comprised all the occult wisdom of things which God has made plainly manifest to men, both by His word and by the creatures of His hands, so that they may have a true knowledge of them. This shall be made more clear in another place.

CHAPTER V

CONCERNING THE CHIEF AND SUPREME ESSENCE OF THINGS

The Magi in their wisdom asserted that all creatures might be brought to one unified substance, which substance they affirm may, by purifications and purgations, attain to so high a degree of subtlety, such divine nature and occult property, as to work wonderful results. For they considered that by returning to the earth, and by a supreme magical separation, a certain perfect substance would come forth, which is at length, by many industrious and prolonged preparations, exalted and raised up above the range of vegetable substances into mineral, above mineral into metallic, and above perfect metallic substances into a perpetual and divine Quintessence,[7] including in itself the essence of all celestial and terrestrial creatures. The Arabs and Greeks, by the occult characters and hieroglyphic descriptions of the Persians and the Egyptians, attained to secret and abstruse mysteries. When these were obtained and partially understood they saw with their own eyes, in the course of experimenting, many wonderful and strange effects. But since the supercelestial operations lay more deeply hidden than their capacity could penetrate, they did not call this a supercelestial arcanum

---

[7] Man was regarded by Paracelsus as himself in a special manner the true Quintessence. After God had created all the elements, stars, and every other created thing, and had disposed them according to His will, He proceeded, lastly, to the forming of man. He extracted the essence out of the four elements into one mass; He extracted also the essence of wisdom, art, and reason out of the stars, and this twofold essence He congested into one mass: which mass Scripture calls the slime of the earth. From that mass two bodies were made – the sidereal and the elementary. These, according to the light of Nature, are called the quintum esse. The mass was extracted, and therein the firmament and the elements were condensed. What was extracted from the four after this manner constituted a fifth. The Quintessence is the nucleus and the place of the essences and properties of all things in the universal world. All nature came into the hand of God – all potency, all property, all essence of the superior and inferior globe. All these had God joined in His hand, and from these He formed man according to His image. – Philosophia Sagax, Lib. I., c. 2.

according to the institution of the Magi, but the arcanum of the Philosophers' Stone according to the counsel and judgment of Pythagoras. Whoever obtained this Stone overshadowed it with various enigmatical figures, deceptive resemblances, comparisons, and fictitious titles, so that its matter might remain occult. Very little or no knowledge of it therefore can be had from them.

CHAPTER VI

CONCERNING THE DIFFERENT ERRORS AS TO ITS DISCOVERY AND KNOWLEDGE

The philosophers have prefixed most occult names to this matter of the Stone, grounded on mere similitudes. Arnold, observing this, says in his "Rosary" that the greatest difficulty is to find out the material of this Stone; for they have called it vegetable, animal, and mineral, but not according to the literal sense, which is well known to such wise men as have had experience of divine secrets and the miracles of this same Stone. For example, Raymond Lully's "Lunaria" may be cited. This gives flowers of admirable virtues familiar to the philosophers themselves; but it was not the intention of those philosophers that you should think they meant thereby any projection upon metals, or that any such preparations should be made; but the abstruse mind of the philosophers had another intention. In like manner, they called their matter by the name of Martagon, to which they applied an occult alchemical operation; when, notwithstanding that name, it denotes nothing more than a hidden similitude. Moreover, no small error has arisen in the liquid of vegetables, with which a good many have sought to coagulate Mercury,[8] and afterwards to convert it with fixatory waters into Luna, since they supposed that he who in this way could coagulate it without the aid of metals would succeed in becoming the chief master. Now, although the liquids of some vegetables do effect this, yet the result is due merely to the resin, fat, and earthy sulphur with which they abound. This attracts to itself the moisture of the Mercury which rises with the substance in the process of coagulation, but without any advantage resulting. I am well assured

[8] All created things proceed from the coagulated, and after coagulation must go on to resolution. From resolution proceed all procreated things. – De Tartaro (fragment). All bodies of minerals are coagulated by salt. – De Natraralibus Aquis, Lib. III., Tract 2.

that no thick and external Sulphur in vegetables is adapted for a perfect projection in Alchemy, as some have found out to their cost. Certain persons have, it is true, coagulated Mercury with the white and milky juice of tittinal, on account of the intense heat which exists therein; and they have called that liquid "Lac Virginis"; yet this is a false basis. The same may be asserted concerning the juice of celandine, although it colours just as though it were endowed with gold. Hence people conceived a vain idea. At a certain fixed time they rooted up this vegetable, from which they sought for a soul or quintessence, wherefrom they might make a coagulating and transmuting tincture. But hence arose nothing save a foolish error.

CHAPTER VII

CONCERNING THE ERRORS OF THOSE WHO SEEK THE STONE IN VEGETABLES

Some alchemists have pressed a juice out of celandine, boiled it to thickness, and put it in the sun, so that it might coagulate into a hard mass, which, being afterwards pounded into a fine black powder, should turn Mercury by projection into Sol. This they also found to be in vain. Others mixed Sal Ammoniac with this powder; others the Colcothar of Vitriol, supposing that they would thus arrive at their desired result. They brought it by their solutions into a yellow water, so that the Sal Ammoniac allowed an entrance of the tincture into the substance of the Mercury. Yet again nothing was accomplished. There are some again who, instead of the abovementioned substances, take the juices of persicaria, bufonaria, dracunculus, the leaves of willow, tithymal, cataputia, flammula, and the like, and shut them up in a glass vessel with Mercury for some days, keeping them in ashes. Thus it comes about that the Mercury is turned into ashes, but deceptively and without any result. These people were misled by the vain rumours of the vulgar, who give it out that he who is able to coagulate Mercury without metals has the entire Magistery, as we have said before. Many, too, have extracted salts, oils, and sulphurs artificially out of vegetables, but quite in vain. Out of such salts, oils, and sulphurs no coagulation of Mercury, or perfect projection, or tincture, can be made. But when the philosophers compare their matter to a certain golden tree of seven boughs, they mean that such matter includes all the seven metals in its sperm, and that in it these lie hidden. On this account they called their matter vegetable, because, as in the case of natural trees, they also in their time produce various flowers. So, too, the matter of the Stone shews most beautiful colours in the production of its flowers.

The comparison, also, is apt, because a certain matter rises out of the philosophical earth, as if it were a thicket of branches and sprouts: like a sponge growing on the earth. They say, therefore, that the fruit of their tree tends towards heaven. So, then, they put forth that the whole thing hinged upon natural vegetables, though not as to its matter, because their stone contains within itself a body, soul, and spirit, as vegetables do.

CHAPTER VIII

CONCERNING THOSE WHO HAVE SOUGHT THE STONE IN ANIMALS

They have also, by a name based only on resemblances, called this matter Lac Virginis, and the Blessed Blood of Rosy Colour, which, nevertheless, suits only the prophets and sons of God. Hence the sophists[9] gathered that this philosophical matter was in the blood of animals or of man. Sometimes, too, because they are nourished by vegetables, others have sought it in hairs, in salt of urine, in rebis; others in hens' eggs, in milk, and in the calx of egg shells, with all of which they thought they would be able to fix Mercury. Some have extracted salt out of foetid urine, supposing that to be the matter of the Stone. Some persons, again, have considered the little stones found in rebis to be the matter. Others have macerated the membranes of eggs in a sharp lixivium, with which they also mixed calcined egg shells as white as snow. To these they have attributed the arcanum of fixation for the transmutation of Mercury. Others, comparing the white of the egg to silver and the yolk to gold, have chosen it for their matter, mixing with it common salt, sal ammoniac, and burnt tartar. These they shut up in a glass vessel, and puri6ed in a *Balneum Maris* until the white matter became as red as blood. This, again, they distilled into a most offensive liquid, utterly useless for the purpose they had in view. Others have purified the white and yolk of eggs; from which has been generated a basilisk. This they burnt to a deep red powder, and sought to tinge with it, as they learnt from the treatise of Cardinal Gilbert. Many, again, have macerated the galls of oxen, mixed with common salt, and distilled this into a liquid, with which they moistened the

---

[9] So acute is the potency of calcined blood, that if it be poured slowly on iron it produces in the first place a whiteness thereon, and then generates rust. – Scholia in Libros de Tartaro. In Lib. II., Tract II.

cementary powders, supposing that, by means of this Magistery, they would tinge their metals. This they called by the name of "a part with a part", and thence came – just nothing. Others have attempted to transmute tutia by the addition of dragon's blood and other substances, and also to change copper and electrum into gold. Others, according to the Venetian Art, as they call it, take twenty lizard-like animals, more or less, shut them up in a vessel, and make them mad with hunger, so that they may devour one another until only one of them survives. This one is then fed with filings of copper or of electrum. They suppose that this animal, simply by the digestion of his stomach, will bring about the desired transmutation. Finally, they burn this animal into a red powder, which they thought must be gold; but they were deceived. Others, again, having burned the fishes called truitas (trouts), have sometimes, upon melting them, found some gold in them; but there is no other reason for it than this: Those fish sometimes in rivers and streams meet with certain small scales and sparks of gold, which they eat. It is seldom, however, that such deceivers are found, and then chiefly in the courts of princes. The matter of the philosophers is not to be sought in animals: this I announce to all. Still, it is evident that the philosophers called their Stone animal, because in their final operations the virtue of this most excellent fiery mystery caused an obscure liquid to exude drop by drop from the matter in their vessels. Hence they predicted that, in the last times, there should come a most pure man upon the earth, by whom the redemption of the world should be brought about; and that this man should send forth bloody drops of a red colour, by means of which he should redeem the world from sin. In the same way, after its own kind, the blood of their Stone freed the leprous metals from their infirmities and contagion. On these grounds, therefore, they supposed they were justified in saying that their Stone was animal. Concerning this mystery Mercurius speaks as follows to King Calid: –

"This mystery it is permitted only to the prophets of God to know. Hence it comes to pass that this Stone is called animal, because in its blood a soul lies hid. It is likewise composed of body, spirit, and soul. For the same reason they called it their microcosm, because it has the likeness of all things in the world, and thence they termed it animal, as Plato named the great world an animal".

CHAPTER IX

CONCERNING THOSE WHO HAVE SOUGHT THE STONE IN MINERALS

Hereto are added the many ignorant men who suppose the stone to be three-fold, and to be hidden in a triple genus, namely, vegetable, animal, and mineral. Hence it is that they have sought for it in minerals. Now, this is far from the opinion of the philosophers. They affirm that their stone is uniformly vegetable, animal, and mineral. Now, here note that Nature has distributed its mineral sperm into various kinds, as, for instance, into sulphurs, salts, boraxes, nitres, ammoniacs, alums, arsenics, atraments, vitriols, tutias, haematites, orpiments, realgars, magnesias, cinnabar, antimony, talc, cachymia, marcasites, etc. In all these Nature has not yet attained to our matter; although in some of the species named it displays itself in a wonderful aspect for the transmutation of imperfect metals that are to be brought to perfection. Truly, long experience and practice with fire shew many and various permutations in the matter of minerals, not only from one colour to another, but from one essence to another, and from imperfection to perfection. And, although Nature has, by means of prepared minerals, reached some perfection, yet philosophers will not have it that the matter of the philosophic stone proceeds out of any of the minerals, although they say that their stone is universal. Hence, then, the sophists take occasion to persecute Mercury himself with various torments, as with sublimations, coagulations, mercurial waters, aquafortis, and the like. All these erroneous ways should be avoided, together with other sophistical preparations of minerals, and the purgations and fixations of spirits and metals. Wherefore all the preparations of the stone, as of Geber, Albertus Magnus, and the rest, are sophistical. Their purgations, cementations, sublimations, distillations, rectifications, circulations, putrefactions, conjunctions, solutions, ascensions, coagulations, calcinations, and incinerations are utterly profitless, both in the tripod, in the athanor, in the reverberatory furnace, in the melting furnace, the accidioneum, in dung, ashes, sand, or what not; and also in the cucurbite, the pelican, retort, phial, fixatory, and the rest. The same opinion must be passed on the sublimation of Mercury by mineral spirits, for the white and the red, as by vitriol, saltpetre, alum, crocuses, etc., concerning all which subjects that sophist, John de Rupescissa, romances in his treatise on the White and Red Philosophic Stone. Taken altogether, these are merely deceitful dreams. Avoid also the particular sophistry of Geber; for example, his sevenfold sublimations or mortifications, and also the revivifications of Mercury, with his preparations of salts of urine, or salts made by a sepulchre, all which things are untrustworthy. Some others have endeavoured to fix Mercury with: the sulphurs of minerals and metals, but have been greatly deceived. It is true I have seen Mercury by this Art, and by such fixations, brought into a metallic body resembling and counterfeiting good silver in all respects; but when brought to the test it has shewn itself to be false.

CHAPTER X

CONCERNING THOSE WHO HAVE SOUGHT THE STONE AND ALSO PARTICULARS IN MINERALS

Some sophists have tried to squeeze out a fixed oil from Mercury seven times sublimed and as often dissolved by means of aquafortis. In this way they attempt to bring imperfect metals to perfection: but they have been obliged to relinquish their vain endeavour. Some have purged vitriol seven times by calcination, solution, and coagulation, with the addition of two parts of sal ammoniac, and by sublimation, so that it might be resolved into a white water, to which they have added a third part of quicksilver, that it might be coagulated by water. Then afterwards they have sublimated the Mercury several times from the vitriol and sal ammoniac, so that it became a stone. This stone they affirmed, being conceived of the vitriol, to be the Red Sulphur of the philosophers, with which they have, by means of solutions and coagulations, made some progress in attaining the stone; but in projection it has all come to nothing. Others have coagulated Mercury by water of alum into a hard mass like alum itself; and this they have fruitlessly fixed with fixatory waters. The sophists propose to themselves very many ways of fixing Mercury, but to no purpose, for therein nothing perfect or constant can be had. It is therefore in vain to add minerals thereto by sophistical processes, since by all of them he is stirred up to greater malice, is rendered more lively, and rather brought to greater impurity than to any kind of perfection. So, then, the philosophers' matter is not to be sought from thence. Mercury is somewhat imperfect; and to bring it to perfection will be very difficult, nay, impossible for any sophist. There is nothing therein that can be stirred up or compelled to perfection. Some have taken arsenic several times sublimated, and frequently dissolved with oil of tartar and coagulated. This they have pretended to fix, and by it to turn copper into silver. This, however, is merely a sophistical whitening, for arsenic cannot be fixed[10] unless the operator be an Artist, and knows well its tingeing spirit. Truly in this respect all the philosophers have slept, vainly attempting to accomplish anything thereby. Whoever, therefore, is ignorant as to this spirit, cannot have any hopes of fixing it, or of giving it that power which would make it capable of the virtue of transmutation. So, then, I give notice to all that the whitening of which I have just now spoken is grounded on a false basis, and that by it the copper is deceitfully whitened, but not changed.

Now the sophists have mixed this counterfeit Venus with twice its weight of Luna, and sold it to the goldsmiths and mint-masters, until at last they have transmuted themselves into false coiners – not only those who sold, but those who bought it. Some sophists instead of white arsenic take red, and this has turned out false art; because, however it is prepared, it proves to be nothing but whiteness.

Some, again, have gone further and dealt with common sulphur, which, being so yellow, they have boiled in vinegar, lixivium, or sharpest wines, for a day and a night, until it became white. Then afterwards they sublimated it from common salt and the calx of eggs, repeating the process several times; yet, still, though white, it has been always combustible. Nevertheless, with this they have endeavoured to fix Mercury and to turn it into gold; but in vain.

---

[10] One recipe for the fixation of arsenic is as follows: – Take equal parts of arsenic and nitre. Place these in a tigillum, set upon coals so that they may begin to boil and to evaporate. Continue till ebullition and evaporation cease, and the substances shall have settled to the bottom of the vessel like fat melting in a frying-pan; then, for the space of an hour and a half (the longer the better), set it apart to settle. Subsequently pour the compound upon marble, and it will acquire a gold colour. In a damp place it will assume the consistency of a fatty fluid. – De Naturalibus Rebus, c. 9. Again: The fixation of arsenic is performed by salt of urine, after which it is converted by itself into an oil. – Chirurgia Minor, Lib. II.

From this, however, comes the most excellent and beautiful cinnabar that I have ever seen. This they propose to fix with the oil of sulphur by cementation and fixation. It does, indeed, give something of an appearance, but still falls short of the desired object. Others have reduced common sulphur to the form of a hepar, boiling it in vinegar with the addition of linseed oil, or laterine oil, or olive oil. They then pour it into a marble mortar, and make it into the form of a hepar, which they have first distilled into a citrine oil with a gentle fire. But they have found to their loss that they could not do anything in the way of transmuting Luna to Sol as they supposed they would be able. As there is an infinite number of metals, so also there is much variety in the preparation of them: I shall not make further mention of these in this place, because each a mould require a special treatise. Beware also of sophisticated oils of vitriol and antimony. Likewise be on your guard against the oils of the metals, perfect or imperfect, as Sol or Luna; because although the operation of these is most potent in the nature of things, yet the true process is known, even at this day, to very few persons. Abstain also from the sophistical preparations of common mercury, arsenic, sulphur, and the like, by sublimation, descension, fixation by vinegar, saltpetre, tartar, vitriol, sal ammoniac, according to the formulas prescribed in the books of the sophists. Likewise avoid the sophisticated tinctures taken from marcasites and crocus of Mars, and also of that sophistication called by the name of "a part with a part", and of fixed Luna and similar trifles. Although they have some superficial appearance of truth, as the fixation of Luna by little labour and industry, still the progress of the preparation is worthless and weak. Being therefore moved with compassion towards the well meaning operators in this art, I have determined to lay open the whole foundation of philosophy in three separate arcana, namely, in one explained by arsenic, in a second by vitriol, and in a third by antimony; by means of which I will teach the true projection upon Mercury and upon the imperfect metals.

CHAPTER XI

CONCERNING THE TRUE AND PERFECT SPECIAL ARCANUM OF ARSENIC FOR THE WHITE TINCTURE

Some persons have written that arsenic is compounded of Mercury and, Sulphur, others of earth and water; but most writers say that it is of the nature of Sulphur. But, however that may be, its nature is such that it transmutes red copper into white. It may also be brought to such a perfect state of preparation as to be able to tinge. But this is not done in the way pointed out by such evil sophists as Geber in "The Sum of Perfection", Albertus Magnus, Aristotle the chemist in "The Book of the Perfect Magistery", Rhasis and Polydorus; for those writers, however many they be, are either themselves in error, or else they write falsely out of sheer envy, and put forth receipts whilst not ignorant of the truth. Arsenic contains within itself three natural spirits. The first is volatile, combustible, corrosive, and penetrating all metals. This spirit whitens Venus and after some days renders it spongy. But this artifice relates only to those who practise the caustic art. The second spirit is crystalline and sweet. The third is a tingeing spirit separated from the others before mentioned. True philosophers seek for these three natural properties in arsenic with a view to the perfect projection of the wise men.[11] But those barbers who practise surgery seek after that sweet and crystalline nature separated from the tingeing spirit for use in the cure of wounds, buboes, carbuncles, anthrax, and other similar ulcers which are not curable save by gentle means. As for that tingeing spirit, however, unless the pure be separated from the

[11] Concerning the kinds of arsenic, it is to be noted that there are those which flow forth from their proper mineral or metal, and are called native arsenics. Next there are arsenics out of metals after their kind. Then there are those made by Art through transmutation. White or crystalline arsenic is the best for medicine Yellow and red arsenic are utilised by chemists for investigating the transmutation of metals, in which arsenic has a special efficacy. – De Naturalibus Rebus, c. 9.

impure in it, the fixed from the volatile, and the secret tincture from the combustible, it will not in any way succeed according to your wish for projection on Mercury, Venus, or any other imperfect metal. All philosophers have hidden this arcanum as a most excellent mystery. This tingeing spirit, separated from the other two as above, you must join to the spirit of Luna, and digest them together for the space of thirty-two days, or until they have assumed a new body. After it has, on the fortieth natural day, been kindled into flame by the heat of the sun, the spirit appears in a bright whiteness, and is endued with a perfect tingeing arcanum. Then it is at length fit for projection, namely, one part of it upon sixteen parts of an imperfect body, according to the sharpness of the preparation. From thence appears shining and most excellent Luna, as though it had been dug from the bowels of the earth.

CHAPTER XII

GENERAL INSTRUCTION CONCERNING THE ARCANUM OF VITRIOL AND THE RED TINCTURE TO BE EXTRACTED FROM IT[12]

Vitriol is a very noble mineral among the rest, and was held always in highest estimation by philosophers, because the Most High God has adorned it with wonderful gifts. They have veiled its arcanum in enigmatical figures like the following: "Thou shalt go to the inner parts of the earth, and by rectification thou shalt find the occult stone, a true medicine". By the earth they understood the Vitriol itself; and by the inner parts of the earth its sweetness and redness, because in the occult part of the Vitriol lies hid a subtle, noble, and most fragrant juice, and a pure oil. The method of its production is not to be approached by calcination or by distillation. For it must not be deprived on any account of its green colour. If it were, it would at the same time lose its arcanum and its power. Indeed, it should be observed at this point that minerals, and also vegetables and other like things which shew greenness without, contain within themselves an oil red like blood, which is their arcanum. Hence it is clear that the distillations of the druggists are useless, vain, foolish, and of no value, because these people do not know how to extract the bloodlike redness from vegetables. Nature herself is wise, and turns all the waters of vegetables to a lemon colour, and after that into an oil which is very red like blood. The reason why this is so slowly accomplished arises from the too great haste of the ignorant operators who distil it, which causes the

[12] The arcanum of vitriol is the oil of vitriol. Thus: after the aquosity has been removed in coction from vitriol, the spirit is elicited by the application of greater heat. The vitriol then comes over pure in the form of water. This water is combined with the caput mortuum left by the process, and on again separating in a balneum maris, the phlegmatic part passes off, and the oil, or the arcanum of vitriol, remains at the bottom of the vessel. – Ibid.

greenness to be consumed. They have not learnt to strengthen Nature with their own powers, which is the mode whereby that noble green colour ought to be rectified into redness of itself. An example of this is white wine digesting itself into a lemon colour; and in process of time the green colour of the grape is of itself turned into the red which underlies the coerulean. The greenness therefore of the vegetables and minerals being lost by the incapacity of the operators, the essence also and spirit of the oil and of the balsam, which is noblest among arcana, will also perish.

CHAPTER XIII

SPECIAL INSTRUCTION CONCERNING THE PROCESS OF VITRIOL FOR THE RED TINCTURE

Vitriol contains within itself many muddy and viscous imperfections. Therefore its greenness[13] must be often extracted with water, and rectified until it puts off all the impurities of earth. When all these rectifications are finished, take care above all that the matter shall not be exposed to the sun, for this turns its greenness pale, and at the same time absorbs the arcanum. Let it be kept covered up in a warm stove so that no dust may defile it. Afterwards let it be digested in a closed glass vessel for the space of several months, or until different colours and deep redness shew themselves. Still you must not suppose that by this process the redness is sufficiently fixed. It must, in addition, be cleansed from the interior and accidental defilements of the earth, in the following manner: – It must be rectified with acetum until the earthy defilement is altogether removed, and the dregs are taken away. This is now the true and best rectification of its tincture, from which the blessed oil is to be extracted. From this tincture, which is carefully enclosed in a glass vessel, an alembic afterwards placed on it and luted so that no spirit may escape, the spirit of this oil must be extracted by distillation over a mild and slow fire. This oil is much pleasanter and sweeter than any aromatic balsam of the drugsellers, being entirely free from all acridity.[14] There will subside in the

[13] So long as the viridity or greenness of vitriol subsists therein, it is of a soft quality and substance. But if it be excocted so that it is deprived of its moisture, it is thereby changed into a hard stone from which even fire can be struck. When the moisture is evaporated from vitriol, the sulphur which it contains predominates over the salt, and the vitriol turns red. – De Pestilitate, Tract I.

[14] The diagnosis of vitriol is concerned with it both in Medicine and Alchemy. In Medicine it is a paramount remedy. In Alchemy it has many additional purposes. The Art of Medicine and Alchemy consists in the preparation of vitriol, for it is worthless in its crude state. It is like unto wood, out of which it is possible to carve anything. Three kinds of oil are

bottom of the cucurbite some very white earth, shining and glittering like snow. This keep, and protect from all dust. This same earth is altogether separated from its redness.

Thereupon follows the greatest arcanum, that is to say, the Supercelestial Marriage of the Soul, consummately prepared and washed by the blood of the lamb, with its own splendid, shining, and purified body. This is the true supercelestial marriage by which life is prolonged to the last and predestined day. In this way, then, the soul and spirit of the Vitriol, which are its blood, are joined with its purified body, that they may be for eternity inseparable. Take, therefore, this our foliated earth in a glass phial. Into it pour gradually its own oil. The body will receive and embrace its soul; since the body is affected with extreme desire for the soul, and the soul is most perfectly delighted with the embrace of the body. Place this conjunction in a furnace of arcana, and keep it there for forty days. When these have expired you will have a most absolute oil of wondrous perfection, in which Mercury and any other of the imperfect metals are turned into gold.

Now let us turn our attention to its multiplication. Take the corporal Mercury, in the proportion of two parts; pour it over three parts, equal in weight, of the aforesaid oil, and let them remain together for forty days. By this proportion of weight and this order the multiplication becomes infinite.

---

extracted from vitriol – a red oil, by distillation in a retort after an alchemistic method, and this is the most acid of all substances, and has also a corrosive quality – also a green and a white oil, distilled from crude vitriol by descension. – De Vitriolo. Nor let it be regarded as absurd that we assign such great virtues to vitriol, for therein resides, secret and hidden, a certain peculiar golden force, not corporeal but spiritual, which excellent and admirable virtue exists in greater potency and certainty therein than it does in gold. When this golden spirit of vitriol is volatilized and separated from its impurities, so that the essence alone remains, it is like unto potable gold. – De Morbis Amentium, Methodus II., c. 1.

CHAPTER XIV

CONCERNING THE SECRETS AND ARCANA OF ANTIMONY, FOR THE RED TINCTURE, WITH A VIEW TO TRANSMUTATION

Antimony is the true bath of gold. Philosophers call it the examiner and the stilanx. Poets say that in this bath Vulcan washed Phoebus, and purified him from all dirt and imperfection. It is produced from the purest and noblest Mercury and Sulphur, under the genus of vitriol, in metallic form and brightness. Some philosophers call it the White Lead of the Wise Men, or simply the Lead. Take, therefore, of Antimony, the very best of its kind, as much as you will. Dissolve this in its own aquafortis, and throw it into cold water, adding a little of the crocus of Mars, so that it may sink to the bottom of the vessel as a sediment, for otherwise it does not throw off its dregs. After it has been dissolved in this way it will have acquired supreme beauty. Let it be placed in a glass vessel, closely fastened on all sides with a very thick lute, or else in a stone bocia, and mix with it some calcined tutia, sublimated to the perfect degree of fire. It must be carefully guarded from liquefying, because with too great heat it breaks the glass. From one pound of this Antimony a sublimation is made, perfected for a space of two days. Place this sublimated substance in a phial that it may touch the water with its third part, in a luted vessel, so that the spirit may not escape. Let it be suspended over the tripod of arcana, and let the work be urged on at first with a slow fire equal to the sun's heat at midsummer. Then at length on the tenth day let it be gradually increased. For with too great heat the glass vessels are broken, and sometimes even the furnace goes to pieces. While the vapour is ascending different colours appear. Let the fire be moderated until a red matter is seen. Afterwards dissolve in very sharp Acetum, and throw away the dregs. Let the Acetum be abstracted and let it be again dissolved in common distilled water. This again must be abstracted, and the sediment distilled with a very strong fire in a glass vessel closely shut. The whole body of the Antimony will ascend as a very red oil, like the colour of a ruby, and will flow into the receiver, drop by drop, with a most fragrant smell and a very sweet taste.[15] This is the supreme arcanum of the philosophers in Antimony, which they account most highly among the arcana of oils. Then, lastly, let the oil of Sol be made in the following way: – Take of the purest Sol as much as you will, and dissolve it in rectified spirit of wine. Let the spirit be abstracted several times, and an equal number of times let it be dissolved again. Let the last solution be kept with the spirit of wine, and circulated for a month. Afterwards let the volatile gold and the spirit of wine be distilled three or four times by means of an alembic, so that it may flow down into the receiver and be brought to its supreme essence. To half an ounce of this dissolved gold let one ounce of the Oil of Antimony be added. This oil embraces it in the heat of the bath, so that it does not easily let it go, even if the spirit of wine be extracted. In this way you will have the supreme mystery and arcanum of Nature, to which scarcely any equal can be assigned in the nature of things. Let these two oils in combination be shut up together in a phial after the manner described, hung on a tripod for a philosophical month, and warmed with a very gentle fire; although, if the fire be regulated in dire proportion this operation is concluded in thirty-one days, and brought to perfection. By this, Mercury and any other imperfect metals acquire the perfection of gold.

[15] Antimony can be made into a pap with the water of vitriol, and then purified by sal ammoniac, and in this manner there may be obtained from it a thick purple or reddish liquor. This is oil of antimony, and it has many virtues. – Chirurgia Magna, Lib. V. Take three pounds of antimony and as much of sal gemmae. Distil them together in a retort for three natural days, and so you will have a red oil, which has incredible healing power in cases of otherwise incurable wounds. – Chirurgia Minor, Tract II., c. 11.

CHAPTER XV

CONCERNING THE PROJECTION TO BE MADE BY THE MYSTERY AND ARCANUM OF ANTIMONY

No precise weight can be assigned in this work of projection, though the tincture itself may be extracted from a certain subject, in a defined proportion, and with fitting appliances. For instance, that Medicine tinges sometimes thirty, forty, occasionally even sixty, eighty, or a hundred parts of the imperfect metal. So, then, the whole business hinges chiefly on the purification of the Medicine and the industry of the operator, and, next, on the greater; or lesser cleanliness and purity of the imperfect body taken in hand. For instance, one Venus is more pure than another; and hence it happens that no one fixed weight can be specified in projection. This alone is worth noting, that if the operator happens to have taken too much of the tincture, he can correct this mistake by adding more of the imperfect metal. But if there be too much of the subject, so that the powers of the tincture are weakened, this error is easily remedied by a cineritium, or by cementations, or by ablutions in crude Antimony. There is nothing at this stage which need delay the operator; only let him put before himself a fact which has been passed over by the philosophers, and by some studiously veiled, namely, that in projections there must be a revivification, that is to say, an animation of imperfect bodies – nay, so to speak, a spiritualisation; concerning which some have said that their metals are no common ones, since they live and have a soul.

ANIMATION IS PRODUCED IN THE FOLLOWING WAY

Take of Venus, wrought into small plates, as much as you will, ten, twenty, or forty pounds. Let these be incrusted with a pulse made of arsenic and calcined tartar, and calcined in their own vessel for twenty-four hours. Then at length let the Venus be pulverised, washed, and thoroughly purified. Let the calcination with ablution be repeated three or four times. In this way it is purged and purified from its thick greenness and from its own impure sulphur. You will have to be on your guard against calcinations made with common sulphur. For whatever is good in the metal is spoilt thereby, and what is bad becomes worse. To ten marks of this purged Venus add one of pure Luna. But in order that the work of the Medicine may be accelerated by projection, and may more easily penetrate the imperfect body, and drive out all portions which are opposed to the nature of Luna, this is accomplished by means of a perfect ferment. For the work is defiled by means of an impure Sulphur, so that a cloud is stretched out over the surface of the transmuted substance, or the metal is mixed with the loppings of the Sulphur and may be cast away therewith. But if a projection of a red stone is to be made, with a view to a red transmutation, it must first fall on gold, afterwards on silver, or on some other metal thoroughly purified, as we have directed above. From thence arises the most perfect gold.

CHAPTER XVI

CONCERNING THE UNIVERSAL MATTER OF THE PHILOSOPHERS' STONE

After the mortification of vegetables, they are transmuted, by the concurrence of two minerals, such as Sulphur and Salt, into a mineral nature, so that at length they themselves become perfect minerals. So it is that in the mineral burrows and caves of the earth, vegetables are found which, in the long succession of time, and by the continuous heat of sulphur, put off the vegetable nature and assume that of the mineral. This happens, for the most part, where the appropriate nutriment is taken away from vegetables of this kind, so that they are afterwards compelled to derive their nourishment from the sulphur and salts of the earth, until what was before vegetable passes over into a perfect mineral. From this mineral state, too, sometimes a perfect metallic essence arises, and this happens by the progress of one degree into another.

But let us return to the Philosophers' Stone. The matter of this, as certain writers have mentioned, is above all else difficult to discover and abstruse to understand. The method and most certain rule for finding out this, as well as other subjects – what they embrace or are able to effect – is a careful examination of the root and seed by which they come to our knowledge. For this, before all things else, a consideration of principles is absolutely necessary; and also of the manner in which Nature proceeds from imperfection to the end of perfection. Now, for this consideration it is well to have it thoroughly understood from the first that all things created by Nature consist of three primal elements, namely, natural Mercury, Sulphur, and Salt in combination, so that in some substances they are volatile, in others fixed. Wherever corporal Salt is mixed with spiritual Mercury and animated Sulphur into one body, then Nature begins to work, in those subterranean places which serve for her vessels, by means of a separating fire. By this the thick and impure Sulphur is separated from the pure, the earth is segregated from the Salt, and the clouds from the Mercury, while those purer parts are preserved, which Nature again welds together into a pure geogamic body. This operation is esteemed by the Magi as a mixture and conjunction by the uniting of three constituents, body, soul, and spirit. When this union is completed there results from it a pure Mercury. Now if this, when flowing down through its subterranean passages and veins, meets with a chaotic Sulphur, the Mercury is coagulated by it according to the condition of the Sulphur. It is, however, still volatile, so that scarcely in a hundred years is it transformed into a metal. Hence arose the vulgar idea that Mercury and Sulphur are the matter of the metals, as is certainly reported by miners. It is not, however, common Mercury and common Sulphur which are the matter of the metals, but the Mercury and the Sulphur of the philosophers are incorporated and inborn in perfect metals, and in the forms of them, so that they never fly from the fire, nor are they depraved by the force of the corruption caused by the elements. It is true that by the dissolution of this natural mixture our Mercury is subdued, as all the philosophers say. Under this form of words our Mercury comes to be drawn from perfect bodies and from the forces of the earthly planets. This is what Hermes asserts in the following terms: "The Sun and the Moon are the roots of this Art". The Son of Hamuel says that the Stone of the philosophers is water coagulated, namely, in Sol and Luna. From this it is clearer than the sun that the material of the Stone is nothing else but Sol and Luna. This is confirmed by the fact that like produces like. We know that there are only two Stones, the white and the red. There are also two matters of the Stone, Sol and Luna, formed together in a proper marriage, both natural and artificial. Now, as we see that the man or the woman, without the seed of both, cannot generate, in the same way our man, Sol, and his wife, Luna, cannot conceive or do an thing in the way of generation, without the seed and sperm of both. Hence the philosophers gathered that a third thing was necessary, namely, the animated seed of both, the man and the woman, without which they judged that the whole of their work was fruitless and in vain. Such a sperm is Mercury, which, by the natural conjunction of both bodies Sol and Luna, receives their nature into itself in union. Then at length, and not before, the work is fit for congress, ingress, and generation; by the masculine and feminine power and virtue. Hence the philosophers have said that this same Mercury is composed of body, spirit, and soul, and that it has assumed the nature and property of all elements. Therefore, with their most powerful genius and intellect, they asserted their Stone to be animal. They even called it their Adam, who carries his own invisible Eve hidden in his body, from that moment in which they were united by the power of the Supreme God, the Maker of all creatures. For this reason it may be said that the Mercury of the Philosophers is none other than their most abstruse, compounded Mercury, and not the common Mercury. So then they have wisely said to the sages that there is in Mercury whatever wise men seek. Almadir, the philosopher, says: "We extract our Mercury from one perfect body and two perfect natural conditions incorporated together, which indeed puts forth externally its perfection, whereby it is able to resist the fire, so that its internal imperfection may be protected by the external perfections". By this passage of the sagacious philosopher is understood the Adamic matter, the limbus of the microcosm,[16] and the homogeneous, unique matter of the philosophers. The sayings of these men, which we have before

[16] Antimony can be made into a pap with the water of vitriol, and then purified by sal ammoniac, and in this manner there may be obtained from it a thick purple or reddish liquor. This is oil of antimony, and it has many virtues. – Chirurgia Magna, Lib. V. Take three pounds of antimony and as much of sal gemmae. Distil them together in a retort for three natural days, and so you will have a red oil, which has incredible healing power in cases of otherwise incurable wounds. – Chirurgia Minor, Tract II., c. 11.

mentioned, are simply golden, and ever to be held in the highest esteem, because they contain nothing superfluous or without force. Summarily, then, the matter of the Philosophers' Stone is none other than a fiery and perfect Mercury extracted by Nature and Art; that is, the artificially prepared and true hermaphrodite Adam, and the microcosm: That wisest of the philosophers, Mercurius, making the same statement, called the Stone an orphan. Our Mercury, therefore, is the same which contains in itself all the perfections, force, and virtues of the Sun, which also runs through all the streets and houses of all the planets, and in its own rebirth has acquired the force of things above and things below; to the marriage of which it is to be compared, as is clear from the whiteness and the redness combined in it.

CHAPTER XVII

CONCERNING THE PREPARATION OF THE MATTER FOR THE PHILOSOPHIC STONE

What Nature principally requires is that its own philosophic man should be brought into a mercurial substance, so that it may be born into the philosophic Stone. Moreover, it should be remarked that those common preparations of Geber, Albertus Magnus, Thomas Aquinas, Rupescissa, Polydorus, and such men, are nothing more than some particular solutions, sublimations, and calcinations, having no reference to our universal substance, which needs only the most secret fire of the philosophers. Let the fire and Azoth therefore suffice for you. From the fact that the philosophers make mention of certain preparations, such as putrefaction, distillation, sublimation, calcination, coagulation, dealbation, rubification, ceration, fixation, and the like, you should understand that in their universal substance, Nature herself fulfils all the operations in the matter spoken of, and not the operator, only in a philosophical vessel, and with a similar fire, but not common fire. The white and the red spring from one root without any intermediary. It is dissolved by itself, it copulates by itself, grows white, grows red, is made crocus-coloured and black by itself, marries itself and conceives in itself. It is therefore to be decocted, to be baked, to be fused; it ascends, and it descends. All these operations are a single operation and produced by the fire alone. Still, some philosophers, nevertheless, have, by a highly graduated essence of wine, dissolved the body of Sol, and rendered it volatile, so that it should ascend through an alembic, thinking that this is the true volatile matter of the philosophers, though it is not so. And although it be no contemptible arcanum to reduce this perfect metallic body into a volatile, spiritual substance, yet they are wrong in their separation of the elements. This process of the monks, such as Lully, Richard of England, Rupescissa, and the rest, is erroneous. By this process they thought that they were going to separate gold after this fashion into a subtle, spiritual, and elementary power, each by itself, and afterwards by circulation and rectification to combine them again in one – but in vain. For although one element may, in a certain sense, be separated from another, yet, nevertheless, every element separated in this way can again be separated into another element, but these elements cannot afterwards by circulation in a pelican, or by distillation, be again brought back into one; but they always remain a certain volatile matter, and aurum potabile, as they themselves call it. The reason why they could not compass their intention is that Nature refuses to be in this way dragged asunder and separated by man's disjunctions, as by earthly glasses and instruments. She alone knows her own operations and the weights of the elements, the separations, rectifications, and copulations of which she brings about without the aid of any operator or manual artifice, provided only the matter be contained in the secret fire and in its proper occult vessel. The separation of the elements, therefore, is impossible by man. It may appear to take place, but it is not true, whatever may be said by Raymond Lully, and of that famous English golden work which he is falsely supposed to have accomplished. Nature herself has within herself the proper separator, who again joins together what he has put asunder, without the aid of man. She knows best the proportion of every element, which man does not know, however misleading writers romance in their frivolous and false recipes about this volatile gold.

This is the opinion of the philosophers, that when they have put their matter into the more secret fire, and when with a moderated philosophical heat it is cherished on every side, beginning to pass into corruption, it grows black. This operation they term putrefaction, and they call the blackness by the name of the Crow's Head. The ascent and descent thereof they term distillation, ascension, and descension. The exsiccation they call coagulation; and the dealbation they call calcination; while because it becomes fluid and soft in the heat they make mention of ceration. When it ceases to ascend and remains liquid at the bottom, they say fixation is present.

In this manner it is the terms of philosophical operations are to bc understood, and not otherwise.

CHAPTER XVIII

CONCERNING INSTRUMENTS AND THE PHILOSOPHIC VESSEL

Sham philosophers have misunderstood the occult and secret philosophic vessel, and worse is that which is said by Aristoteles the Alchemist (not the famous Greek Academic Philosopher), giving it out that the matter is to be decocted in a triple vessel. Worst of all is that which is said by another, namely, that the matter in its first separation and first degree requires a metallic vessel; in its second degree of coagulation and dealbation of its earth a glass vessel; and in the third degree, for fixation, an earthen vessel. Nevertheless, hereby the philosophers understand one vessel alone in all the operations up to the perfection of the red stone. Since, then, our matter is our root for the white and the red, necessarily our vessel must be so fashioned that the matter in it may be governed by the heavenly bodies. For invisible celestial influences and the impressions of the stars are in the very first degree necessary for the work: Otherwise it would be impossible for the Oriental, Chaldean, and Egyptian stone to be realised. By this Anaxagoras knew the powers of the whole firmament, and foretold that a great stone would descend from heaven to earth, which actually happened after his death. To the Cabalists our vessel is perfectly well known, because it must be made according to a truly geometrical proportion and measure, and from a definite quadrature of the circle, so that the spirit and the soul of our matter, separated from their body, may be able to raise this vessel with themselves in proportion to the altitude of heaven. If the vessel be wider, narrower, higher, or lower than is fitting, and than the dominating operating spirit and soul desire, the heat of our secret philosophic fire (which is, indeed, very severe), will violently excite the matter and urge it on to excessive operation, so that the vessel is shivered into a thousand pieces, with imminent danger to the body and even the life of the operator. On the other hand, if it be of greater capacity than is required in due proportion for the heat to have effect on the matter, the work will be wasted and thrown away. So, then, our philosophic vessel must be made with the greatest care. What the material of the vessel should be is understood only by those who, in the first solution of our fixed and perfected matter have brought that matter to its own primal quintessence. Enough has been said on this point.

The operator must also very accurately note what, in its first solution, the matter sends forth and rejects from itself.

The method of describing the form of the vessel is difficult. It should be such as Nature requires, and it must be sought out and investigated from every possible source, so that, from the height of the philosophic heaven, elevated above the philosophic earth, it may be able to operate on the fruit of its own earthly body. It should have this form, too, in order that the separation and purification of the elements, when the fire drives one from the other, may be able to be accomplished, and that each may have power to occupy the place to which it adheres; and also that the sun and the other planets may exercise their operations around the elemental earth, while their course in their circuit is neither hindered nor agitated with too swift a motion. In all these particulars which have been mentioned it must have a proper proportion of rotundity and of height.

The instruments for the first purification of mineral bodies are fusing-vessels, bellows, tongs, capels, cupels, tests, cementatory vessels, cineritiums, cucurbites, bocias for aquafortis and aqua regia; and also the appliances which are required for projection at the climax of the work.

CHAPTER XIX

CONCERNING THE SECRET FIRE OF THE PHILOSOPHERS

This is a well-known sententious saying of the philosophers, "Let fire and Azoc suffice thee". Fire alone is the whole work and the entire art. Moreover, they who build their fire and keep their vessel in that heat are in error. In vain some have attempted it with the heat of horse dung. By the coal fire, without a medium, they have sublimated their matter, but they have not dissolved it. Others have got their heat from lamps, asserting that this is the secret fire of the philosophers for making their Stone. Some have placed it in a bath, first of all in heaps of ants' eggs; others in juniper ashes. Some have sought the fire in quicklime, in tartar, vitriol, nitre, etc. Others, again, have sought it in boiling water. Thomas Aquinas speaks falsely of this fire, saying that God and the angels cannot do without this fire, but use it daily. What blasphemy is this! Is it not a manifest lie that God is not able to do without the elemental heat of boiling water? All the heats excited by those means which have been mentioned are utterly useless for our work Take care not to be misled by Arnold de Villa Nova, who has written on the subject of the coal fire, for in this matter he will deceive you.

Almadir says that the invisible rays of our fire of themselves suffice. Another cites, as an illustration, that the heavenly heat by its reflections tends to the coagulation and perfection of Mercury, just as by its continual motion it tends to the generation of metals. Again, says this same authority, "Make a fire, vaporous, digesting, as for cooking, continuous, but not volatile or boiling, enclosed, shut off from the air, not burning, but altering and penetrating. Now, in truth, I have mentioned every mode of fire and of exciting heat. If you are a true philosopher you will understand". This is what he says.

Salmanazar remarks: "Ours is a corrosive fire, which brings over our vessel an air like a cloud, in which cloud the rays of this fire are hidden. If this dew of chaos and this moisture of the cloud fail, a mistake has been committed". Again, Almadir says, that unless the fire has warmed our sun with its moisture, by the excrement of the mountain, with a moderate ascent, we shall not be partakers either of the Red or the White Stone.

All these matters shew quite openly to us the occult fire of the wise men. Finally, this is the matter of our fire, namely, that it be kindled by the quiet spirit of sensible fire, which drives upwards, as it were, the heated chaos from the opposite quarter, and above our philosophic matter. This heat, glowing above our vessel, must urge it to the motion of a perfect generation, temperately but continuously, without intermission.

CHAPTER XX

CONCERNING THE FERMENT OF THE PHILOSOPHERS, AND THE WEIGHT

Philosophers have laboured greatly in the art of ferments and of fermentations, which seems important above all others. With reference thereto some have made a vow to God and to the philosophers that they would never divulge its arcanum by similitudes or by parables.

Nevertheless, Hermes, the father of all philosophers, in the "Book of the Seven Treatises", most clearly discloses the secret of ferments, saying that they consist only of their own paste; and more at length he says that the ferment whitens the confection, hinders combustion, altogether retards the flux of the tincture, consoles bodies, and amplifies unions. He says, also, that this is the key and the end of the work, concluding that the ferment is nothing but paste, as that of the sun is nothing but sun, and that of the moon nothing but moon. Others affirm that the ferment is the soul, and if this be not rightly prepared from the magistery, it effects nothing. Some zealots of this Art seek the Art in common sulphur, arsenic, tutia, auripigment, vitriol, etc., but in vain; since the substance which is sought is the same as that from which it has to be drawn forth. It should be remarked, therefore, that fermentations of this kind do not succeed according to the wishes of the zealots in the way they desire, but, as is clear from what has been said above, simply in the way of natural successes.

But, to come at length to the weight; this must be noted in two ways. The first is natural, the second artificial. The natural attains its result in the earth by Nature and concordance. Of this, Arnold says: If more or less earth than Nature requires be added, the soul is suffocated, and no result is perceived, nor any fixation. It is the same with the water. If more or less of this bc taken it will bring a corresponding loss. A superfluity renders the matter unduly moist, and a deficiency makes it too dry and too hard. If there be over much air present, it is too strongly impressed on the tincture; if there be too little, the body will turn out pallid. In the same way, if the fire be too strong, the matter is burnt up; if it be too slack, it has not the power of drying, nor of dissolving or heating the other elements. In these things elemental heat consists.

Artificial weight is quite occult. It is comprised in the magical art of ponderations. Between the spirit, soul, and body, say the philosophers, weight consists of Sulphur as the director of the work; for the soul strongly desires Sulphur, and necessarily observes it by reason of its weight.

You can understand it thus: Our matter is united to a red fixed Sulphur, to which a third part of the regimen has been entrusted, even to the ultimate degree, so that it may perfect to infinity the operation of the Stone, may remain therewith together with its fire, and may consist of a weight equal to the matter itself, in and through all, without variation of any degree. Therefore, after the matter has been adapted and mixed in its proportionate weight, it should be closely shut up with its seal in the vessel of the philosophers, and committed to the secret fire. In this the Philosophic Sun will rise and surge up, and will illuminate all things that have been looking for his light, expecting it with highest hope.

In these few words we will conclude the arcanum of the Stone, an arcanum which is in no way maimed or defective, for which we give God undying thanks. Now have we opened to you our treasure, which is not to be paid for by the riches of the whole world.

HERE ENDS THE AURORA OF THE PHILOSOPHERS

www.ingramcontent.com/pod-product-compliance
Lightning Source LLC
LaVergne TN
LVHW050946080826
845145LV00004B/1424

* 9 7 8 1 6 3 1 1 8 5 0 7 6 *